Fill My Recipe Book

Thank you for purchasing this blank recipe book!

I hope it collects many treasured recipes.

- - - -

Find ideas to fill your new recipe book on my blog
www.FillMyRecipeBook.com

- - - -

TIP: The Notes section of each recipe is also a great place
to include a URL, magazine or book name you got a new recipe from
so that you can revisit if needed.

Dry Volume Measurements

1 teaspoon	-	5ml
1 tablespoon	-	15ml
2 tablespoons	-	30ml
¼ cup	-	60ml
⅓ cup	-	75ml
½ cup	-	125ml
⅔ cup	-	150ml
¾ cup	-	175ml
1 cup	-	250ml
2 cups / 1 pint	-	500ml
3 cups	-	750ml
4 cups / 1 quart	-	1 L

Fluid Volume Measurements

1 ounce	2 tablespoons	30ml
4 ounce	½ cup	125ml
8 ounce	1 cup	250ml
12 ounce	1 ½ cups	375ml
16 ounces	2 cups	500ml

Mass Dry Weights

½ ounce	15g
1 ounce	30g
3 ounces	90g
4 ounces	120g
8 ounces	225g
10 ounces	285g
12 ounces	360g
16 ounces / 1 pound	450g

Measurements

cup	tablespoons	teaspoons
1	16	48
¾	12	36
⅔	10 ⅔	32
½	8	24
⅓	5 ⅓	16
¼	4	12
⅛	2	6
1/16th	1	3

Oven Temperatures

250 °F	-	120 °C
275 °F	-	140 °C
300 °F	-	150 °C
325 °F	-	160 °C
350 °F	-	180 °C
375 °F	-	190 °C
400 °F	-	200 °C
425 °F	-	220 °C
450 °F	-	230 °C

Helpful Tips

1 packet of yeast	2 ½ teaspoons yeast
1 lemon	2 tablespoons lemon juice
1 cup Buttermilk	1 tablespoon vinegar or lemon juice plus milk to make 1 cup. let sit 10 minutes

Recipe Index

Recipe Type:

Page	Recipe Name		Page	Recipe Name
10			35	
11			36	
12			37	
13			38	
14			39	
15			40	
16			41	
17			42	
18			43	
19			44	
20			45	
21			46	
22			47	
23			48	
24			49	
25			50	
26			51	
27			52	
28			53	
29			54	
30			55	
31			56	
32			57	
33			58	
34			59	

Recipe Type:

Page	Recipe Name
62	
63	
64	
65	
66	
67	
68	
69	
70	
71	
72	
73	
74	
75	
76	
77	
78	
79	
80	
81	
82	
83	
84	
85	
86	
87	
88	

Page	Recipe Name
89	
90	
91	
92	
93	
94	
95	
96	
97	
98	
99	
100	
101	
102	
103	
104	
105	
106	
107	
108	
109	
110	
111	
112	
113	
114	
115	

Recipe Type:

Page	Recipe Name	Page	Recipe Name
118		145	
119		146	
120		147	
121		148	
122		149	
123		150	
124		151	
125		152	
126		153	
127		154	
128		155	
129		156	
130		157	
131		158	
132		159	
133		160	
134		161	
135		162	
136		163	
137		164	
138		165	
139		166	
140		167	
141		168	
142		169	
143		170	
144		171	

Recipe Type:

Page	Recipe Name
174	
175	
176	
177	
178	
179	
180	
181	
182	
183	
184	
185	
186	
187	
188	
189	
190	
191	
192	
193	
194	
195	
196	
197	
198	
199	

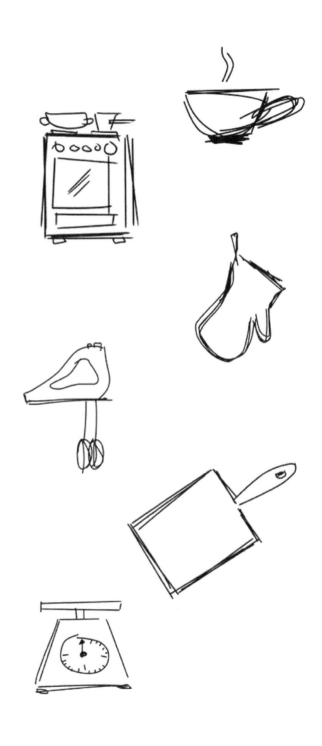

Let Food be thy Medicine, and let thy Medicine be Food
- Hippocrates

Recipe Name: _____ ☆☆☆☆☆

Nutrition Info

Serves
Prep Time
Oven Temp
Cook Time

Ingredients

Directions

Notes:

Recipe Name: _____ ☆☆☆☆☆

Nutrition Info

Serves
Prep Time
Oven Temp
Cook Time

Ingredients

Directions

Notes:

Recipe Name: _____ ☆☆☆☆☆

Nutrition Info

Serves
Prep Time
Oven Temp
Cook Time

Ingredients

Directions

Notes:

Recipe Name: _____ ☆☆☆☆☆

Nutrition Info   Serves
                                                     Prep Time
                                                    Oven Temp
                                                    Cook Time

Ingredients   # Directions

Notes:

Recipe Name: _____ ☆☆☆☆☆

Nutrition Info

Serves
Prep Time
Oven Temp
Cook Time

Ingredients

Directions

Notes:

Recipe Name: _____ ☆☆☆☆☆

Nutrition Info

Serves
Prep Time
Oven Temp
Cook Time

Ingredients

Directions

Notes:

Recipe Name: _____ ☆☆☆☆☆

Nutrition Info

Serves
Prep Time
Oven Temp
Cook Time

Ingredients

Directions

Notes:

Recipe Name: _____ ☆☆☆☆☆

Nutrition Info

Serves
Prep Time
Oven Temp
Cook Time

Ingredients

Directions

Notes:

Recipe Name: _____ ☆☆☆☆☆

Nutrition Info

Serves
Prep Time
Oven Temp
Cook Time

Ingredients

Directions

Notes:

Recipe Name: _____

☆☆☆☆☆

Nutrition Info

Serves
Prep Time
Oven Temp
Cook Time

Ingredients

Directions

Notes:

Recipe Name: _____ ☆☆☆☆☆

Nutrition Info

Serves
Prep Time
Oven Temp
Cook Time

Ingredients

Directions

Notes:

Recipe Name: _____ ☆☆☆☆☆

Nutrition Info

Serves
Prep Time
Oven Temp
Cook Time

Ingredients

Directions

Notes:

Recipe Name: _____ ☆☆☆☆☆

Nutrition Info

Serves
Prep Time
Oven Temp
Cook Time

Ingredients

Directions

Notes:

Recipe Name: _____ ☆☆☆☆☆

Nutrition Info

Serves
Prep Time
Oven Temp
Cook Time

Ingredients

Directions

Notes:

Recipe Name: _____ ☆☆☆☆☆

Nutrition Info

Serves
Prep Time
Oven Temp
Cook Time

Ingredients

Directions

Notes:

Recipe Name: _____ ☆☆☆☆☆

Nutrition Info

Serves
Prep Time
Oven Temp
Cook Time

Ingredients

Directions

Notes:

Recipe Name: _____ ☆☆☆☆☆

Nutrition Info

Serves
Prep Time
Oven Temp
Cook Time

Ingredients

Directions

Notes:

Recipe Name: _____ ☆☆☆☆☆

Nutrition Info

Serves
Prep Time
Oven Temp
Cook Time

Ingredients

Directions

Notes:

Recipe Name: _____ ☆☆☆☆☆

Nutrition Info

Serves

Prep Time

Oven Temp

Cook Time

Ingredients

Directions

Notes:

Recipe Name: _____ ☆☆☆☆☆

Nutrition Info

Serves

Prep Time

Oven Temp

Cook Time

Ingredients

Directions

Notes:

Recipe Name: _____ ☆☆☆☆☆

Nutrition Info

Serves
Prep Time
Oven Temp
Cook Time

Ingredients

Directions

Notes:

Recipe Name: _____ ☆☆☆☆☆

Nutrition Info

Serves
Prep Time
Oven Temp
Cook Time

Ingredients

Directions

Notes:

Recipe Name: _____ ☆☆☆☆☆

Nutrition Info

Serves
Prep Time
Oven Temp
Cook Time

Ingredients

Directions

Notes:

Recipe Name: _____

☆☆☆☆☆

Nutrition Info

Serves
Prep Time
Oven Temp
Cook Time

Ingredients

Directions

Notes:

Recipe Name: _____ ☆☆☆☆☆

Nutrition Info

Serves
Prep Time
Oven Temp
Cook Time

Ingredients

Directions

Notes:

Recipe Name: _____ ☆☆☆☆☆

Nutrition Info

Serves
Prep Time
Oven Temp
Cook Time

Ingredients

Directions

Notes:

Recipe Name: _____ ☆☆☆☆☆

Nutrition Info

Serves
Prep Time
Oven Temp
Cook Time

Ingredients

Directions

Notes:

Recipe Name: _____ ☆☆☆☆☆

Nutrition Info

Serves
Prep Time
Oven Temp
Cook Time

Ingredients

Directions

Notes:

Recipe Name: _____ ☆☆☆☆☆

Nutrition Info

Serves
Prep Time
Oven Temp
Cook Time

Ingredients

Directions

Notes:

Recipe Name: _____ ☆☆☆☆☆

Nutrition Info

Serves
Prep Time
Oven Temp
Cook Time

Ingredients

Directions

Notes:

Recipe Name: _____ ☆☆☆☆☆

Nutrition Info

Serves
Prep Time
Oven Temp
Cook Time

Ingredients

Directions

Notes:

Recipe Name: _____ ☆☆☆☆☆

Nutrition Info

Serves
Prep Time
Oven Temp
Cook Time

Ingredients

Directions

Notes:

Recipe Name: _____ ☆☆☆☆☆

Nutrition Info

Serves
Prep Time
Oven Temp
Cook Time

Ingredients

Directions

Notes:

Recipe Name: _____ ☆☆☆☆☆

Nutrition Info

Serves
Prep Time
Oven Temp
Cook Time

Ingredients

Directions

Notes:

Recipe Name: _____ ☆☆☆☆☆

Nutrition Info

Serves
Prep Time
Oven Temp
Cook Time

Ingredients

Directions

Notes:

Recipe Name: _____ ☆☆☆☆☆

Nutrition Info

Serves
Prep Time
Oven Temp
Cook Time

Ingredients

Directions

Notes:

Recipe Name: _____ ☆☆☆☆☆

Nutrition Info

Serves
Prep Time
Oven Temp
Cook Time

Ingredients

Directions

Notes:

Recipe Name: _____ ☆☆☆☆☆

Nutrition Info

Serves
Prep Time
Oven Temp
Cook Time

Ingredients

Directions

Notes:

Recipe Name: _____ ☆☆☆☆☆

Nutrition Info

Serves
Prep Time
Oven Temp
Cook Time

Ingredients

Directions

Notes:

Recipe Name: _____ ☆☆☆☆☆

Nutrition Info

Serves
Prep Time
Oven Temp
Cook Time

Ingredients

Directions

Notes:

Recipe Name: _____ ☆☆☆☆☆

Nutrition Info

Serves
Prep Time
Oven Temp
Cook Time

Ingredients

Directions

Notes:

Recipe Name: _____ ☆☆☆☆☆

Nutrition Info

Serves
Prep Time
Oven Temp
Cook Time

Ingredients

Directions

Notes:

Recipe Name: _____ ☆☆☆☆☆

Nutrition Info

Serves
Prep Time
Oven Temp
Cook Time

Ingredients

Directions

Notes:

Recipe Name: _____ ☆☆☆☆☆

Nutrition Info

Serves
Prep Time
Oven Temp
Cook Time

Ingredients

Directions

Notes:

Recipe Name: _____ ☆☆☆☆☆

Nutrition Info

Serves
Prep Time
Oven Temp
Cook Time

Ingredients

Directions

Notes:

Recipe Name: _____ ☆☆☆☆☆

Nutrition Info

Serves
Prep Time
Oven Temp
Cook Time

Ingredients

Directions

Notes:

Recipe Name: _____ ☆☆☆☆☆

Nutrition Info

Serves
Prep Time
Oven Temp
Cook Time

Ingredients

Directions

Notes:

Recipe Name: _____ ☆☆☆☆☆

Nutrition Info

Serves
Prep Time
Oven Temp
Cook Time

Ingredients

Directions

Notes:

Recipe Name: _____ ☆☆☆☆☆

Nutrition Info

Serves
Prep Time
Oven Temp
Cook Time

Ingredients

Directions

Notes:

Recipe Name: _____ ☆☆☆☆☆

Nutrition Info   Serves
                                                  Prep Time
                                                  Oven Temp
                                                  Cook Time

Ingredients   ## Directions

Notes:

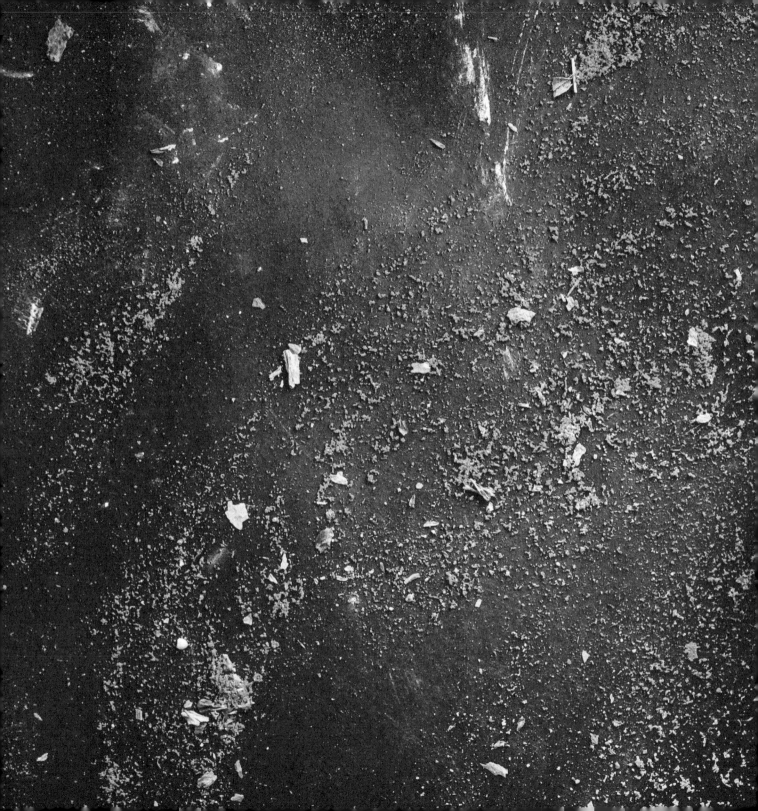

Recipe Name: _____ ☆☆☆☆☆

Nutrition Info

Serves
Prep Time
Oven Temp
Cook Time

Ingredients

Directions

Notes:

Recipe Name: _____ ☆☆☆☆☆

Nutrition Info

Serves
Prep Time
Oven Temp
Cook Time

Ingredients

Directions

Notes:

Recipe Name: _____ ☆ ☆ ☆ ☆ ☆

Nutrition Info

Serves
Prep Time
Oven Temp
Cook Time

Ingredients

Directions

Notes:

Recipe Name: _____ ☆☆☆☆☆

Nutrition Info

Serves
Prep Time
Oven Temp
Cook Time

Ingredients

Directions

Notes:

Recipe Name: _____ ☆☆☆☆☆

Nutrition Info

Serves
Prep Time
Oven Temp
Cook Time

Ingredients

Directions

Notes:

Recipe Name: _____ ☆☆☆☆☆

Nutrition Info

Serves
Prep Time
Oven Temp
Cook Time

Ingredients

Directions

Notes:

Recipe Name: _____ ☆☆☆☆☆

Nutrition Info

Serves
Prep Time
Oven Temp
Cook Time

Ingredients

Directions

Notes:

Recipe Name: _____ ☆☆☆☆☆

Nutrition Info

Serves
Prep Time
Oven Temp
Cook Time

Ingredients

Directions

Notes:

Recipe Name: _____ ☆☆☆☆☆

Nutrition Info

Serves
Prep Time
Oven Temp
Cook Time

Ingredients

Directions

Notes:

Recipe Name: _____ ☆☆☆☆☆

Nutrition Info

Serves
Prep Time
Oven Temp
Cook Time

Ingredients

Directions

Notes:

Recipe Name: _____ ☆☆☆☆☆

Nutrition Info

Serves
Prep Time
Oven Temp
Cook Time

Ingredients

Directions

Notes:

Recipe Name: _____ ☆☆☆☆☆

Nutrition Info

Serves
Prep Time
Oven Temp
Cook Time

Ingredients

Directions

Notes:

Recipe Name: _____ ☆☆☆☆☆

Nutrition Info

Serves
Prep Time
Oven Temp
Cook Time

Ingredients

Directions

Notes:

Recipe Name: _____ ☆☆☆☆☆

Nutrition Info

Serves
Prep Time
Oven Temp
Cook Time

Ingredients

Directions

Notes:

Recipe Name: _____ ☆☆☆☆☆

Nutrition Info

Serves
Prep Time
Oven Temp
Cook Time

Ingredients

Directions

Notes:

Recipe Name: _____ ☆☆☆☆☆

Nutrition Info

Serves
Prep Time
Oven Temp
Cook Time

Ingredients

Directions

Notes:

Recipe Name: _____ ☆☆☆☆☆

Nutrition Info

Serves
Prep Time
Oven Temp
Cook Time

Ingredients

Directions

Notes:

Recipe Name: _____ ☆☆☆☆☆

Nutrition Info

Serves
Prep Time
Oven Temp
Cook Time

Ingredients

Directions

Notes:

Recipe Name: _____ ☆☆☆☆☆

Nutrition Info

Serves
Prep Time
Oven Temp
Cook Time

Ingredients

Directions

Notes:

Recipe Name: _____ ☆☆☆☆☆

Nutrition Info

Serves
Prep Time
Oven Temp
Cook Time

Ingredients

Directions

Notes:

Recipe Name: _____ ☆☆☆☆☆

Nutrition Info

Serves
Prep Time
Oven Temp
Cook Time

Ingredients

Directions

Notes:

Recipe Name: _____ ☆☆☆☆☆

Nutrition Info

Serves
Prep Time
Oven Temp
Cook Time

Ingredients

Directions

Notes:

Recipe Name: _____ ☆☆☆☆☆

Nutrition Info

Serves
Prep Time
Oven Temp
Cook Time

Ingredients

Directions

Notes:

Recipe Name: _____ ☆☆☆☆☆

Nutrition Info

Serves
Prep Time
Oven Temp
Cook Time

Ingredients

Directions

Notes:

Recipe Name: _____ ☆☆☆☆☆

Nutrition Info

Serves
Prep Time
Oven Temp
Cook Time

Ingredients

Directions

Notes:

Recipe Name: _____

☆☆☆☆☆

Nutrition Info

Serves
Prep Time
Oven Temp
Cook Time

Ingredients

Directions

Notes:

Recipe Name: _____ ☆☆☆☆☆

Nutrition Info

Serves
Prep Time
Oven Temp
Cook Time

Ingredients

Directions

Notes:

Recipe Name: _____ ☆☆☆☆☆

Nutrition Info

Serves
Prep Time
Oven Temp
Cook Time

Ingredients

Directions

Notes:

Recipe Name: _____ ☆☆☆☆☆

Nutrition Info

Serves
Prep Time
Oven Temp
Cook Time

Ingredients

Directions

Notes:

Recipe Name: _____ ☆☆☆☆☆

Nutrition Info

Serves
Prep Time
Oven Temp
Cook Time

Ingredients

Directions

Notes:

Recipe Name: _____ ☆☆☆☆☆

Nutrition Info

Serves
Prep Time
Oven Temp
Cook Time

Ingredients

Directions

Notes:

Recipe Name: _____ ☆☆☆☆☆

Nutrition Info

Serves
Prep Time
Oven Temp
Cook Time

Ingredients

Directions

Notes:

Recipe Name: _____ ☆☆☆☆☆

Nutrition Info

Serves
Prep Time
Oven Temp
Cook Time

Ingredients

Directions

Notes:

Recipe Name: _____ ☆☆☆☆☆

Nutrition Info

Serves

Prep Time

Oven Temp

Cook Time

Ingredients

Directions

Notes:

Recipe Name: _____ ☆☆☆☆☆

Nutrition Info

Serves
Prep Time
Oven Temp
Cook Time

Ingredients

Directions

Notes:

Recipe Name: _____ ☆☆☆☆☆

Nutrition Info

Serves
Prep Time
Oven Temp
Cook Time

Ingredients

Directions

Notes:

Recipe Name: _____ ☆☆☆☆☆

Nutrition Info

Serves
Prep Time
Oven Temp
Cook Time

Ingredients

Directions

Notes:

Recipe Name: _____ ☆☆☆☆☆

Nutrition Info

Serves
Prep Time
Oven Temp
Cook Time

Ingredients

Directions

Notes:

Recipe Name: _____ ☆☆☆☆☆

Nutrition Info

Serves
Prep Time
Oven Temp
Cook Time

Ingredients

Directions

Notes:

Recipe Name: _____ ☆☆☆☆☆

Nutrition Info

Serves
Prep Time
Oven Temp
Cook Time

Ingredients

Directions

Notes:

Recipe Name: _____ ☆☆☆☆☆

Nutrition Info

Serves
Prep Time
Oven Temp
Cook Time

Ingredients

Directions

Notes:

Recipe Name: _____ ☆☆☆☆☆

Nutrition Info

Serves
Prep Time
Oven Temp
Cook Time

Ingredients

Directions

Notes:

Recipe Name: _____ ☆☆☆☆☆

Nutrition Info

Serves

Prep Time

Oven Temp

Cook Time

Ingredients

Directions

Notes:

Recipe Name: _____ ☆☆☆☆☆

Nutrition Info

Serves
Prep Time
Oven Temp
Cook Time

Ingredients

Directions

Notes:

Recipe Name: _____ ☆☆☆☆☆

Nutrition Info

Serves
Prep Time
Oven Temp
Cook Time

Ingredients

Directions

Notes:

Recipe Name: _____ ☆☆☆☆☆

Nutrition Info

Serves
Prep Time
Oven Temp
Cook Time

Ingredients

Directions

Notes:

Recipe Name: _____ ☆☆☆☆☆

Nutrition Info

Serves
Prep Time
Oven Temp
Cook Time

Ingredients

Directions

Notes:

Recipe Name: _____ ☆☆☆☆☆

Nutrition Info

Serves
Prep Time
Oven Temp
Cook Time

Ingredients

Directions

Notes:

Recipe Name: _____

☆☆☆☆☆

Nutrition Info

Serves
Prep Time
Oven Temp
Cook Time

Ingredients

Directions

Notes:

Recipe Name: _____ ☆☆☆☆☆

Nutrition Info

Serves
Prep Time
Oven Temp
Cook Time

Ingredients

Directions

Notes:

Recipe Name: _____

☆☆☆☆☆

Nutrition Info

Serves
Prep Time
Oven Temp
Cook Time

Ingredients

Directions

Notes:

Recipe Name: _____ ☆☆☆☆☆

Nutrition Info

Serves
Prep Time
Oven Temp
Cook Time

Ingredients

Directions

Notes:

Recipe Name: _____ ☆☆☆☆☆

Nutrition Info

Serves

Prep Time

Oven Temp

Cook Time

Ingredients

Directions

Notes:

Recipe Name: _____ ☆☆☆☆☆

Nutrition Info

Serves
Prep Time
Oven Temp
Cook Time

Ingredients

Directions

Notes:

- The Kitchen is the Heart of the Home -

Recipe Name: _____ ☆☆☆☆☆

Nutrition Info

Serves
Prep Time
Oven Temp
Cook Time

Ingredients

Directions

Notes:

Recipe Name: _____ ☆☆☆☆☆

Nutrition Info

Serves
Prep Time
Oven Temp
Cook Time

Ingredients

Directions

Notes:

Recipe Name: _____ ☆☆☆☆☆

Nutrition Info

Serves
Prep Time
Oven Temp
Cook Time

Ingredients

Directions

Notes:

Recipe Name: _____ ☆☆☆☆☆

Nutrition Info

Serves
Prep Time
Oven Temp
Cook Time

Ingredients

Directions

Notes:

Recipe Name: _____ ☆☆☆☆☆

Nutrition Info

Serves
Prep Time
Oven Temp
Cook Time

Ingredients

Directions

Notes:

Recipe Name: _____ ☆☆☆☆☆

Nutrition Info

Serves
Prep Time
Oven Temp
Cook Time

Ingredients

Directions

Notes:

Recipe Name: _____ ☆☆☆☆☆

Nutrition Info

Serves

Prep Time

Oven Temp

Cook Time

Ingredients

Directions

Notes:

Recipe Name: _____ ☆☆☆☆☆

Nutrition Info

Serves
Prep Time
Oven Temp
Cook Time

Ingredients

Directions

Notes:

Recipe Name: _____ ☆☆☆☆☆

Nutrition Info

Serves
Prep Time
Oven Temp
Cook Time

Ingredients

Directions

Notes:

Recipe Name: _____ ☆☆☆☆☆

Nutrition Info

Serves
Prep Time
Oven Temp
Cook Time

Ingredients

Directions

Notes:

Recipe Name: _____ ☆☆☆☆☆

Nutrition Info

Serves

Prep Time

Oven Temp

Cook Time

Ingredients

Directions

Notes:

Recipe Name: _____ ☆☆☆☆☆

Nutrition Info

Serves
Prep Time
Oven Temp
Cook Time

Ingredients

Directions

Notes:

Recipe Name: _____ ☆☆☆☆☆

Nutrition Info

Serves
Prep Time
Oven Temp
Cook Time

Ingredients

Directions

Notes:

Recipe Name: _____ ☆☆☆☆☆

Nutrition Info

Serves
Prep Time
Oven Temp
Cook Time

Ingredients

Directions

Notes:

Recipe Name: _____ ☆☆☆☆☆

Nutrition Info

Serves
Prep Time
Oven Temp
Cook Time

Ingredients

Directions

Notes: _____

Recipe Name: _____ ☆☆☆☆☆

Nutrition Info

| Serves |
| Prep Time |
| Oven Temp |
| Cook Time |

Ingredients

Directions

Notes:

Recipe Name: _____ ☆☆☆☆☆

Nutrition Info

Serves
Prep Time
Oven Temp
Cook Time

Ingredients

Directions

Notes:

Recipe Name: _____ ☆☆☆☆☆

Nutrition Info

Serves
Prep Time
Oven Temp
Cook Time

Ingredients

Directions

Notes:

Recipe Name: ☆☆☆☆☆

Nutrition Info

Serves
Prep Time
Oven Temp
Cook Time

Ingredients

Directions

Notes:

Recipe Name: _____ ☆☆☆☆☆

Nutrition Info

Serves
Prep Time
Oven Temp
Cook Time

Ingredients

Directions

Notes:

Recipe Name: _____ ☆☆☆☆☆

Nutrition Info

Serves
Prep Time
Oven Temp
Cook Time

Ingredients

Directions

Notes:

Recipe Name: _____ ☆☆☆☆☆

Nutrition Info

Serves
Prep Time
Oven Temp
Cook Time

Ingredients

Directions

Notes:

Recipe Name: _____ ☆☆☆☆☆

Nutrition Info

Serves
Prep Time
Oven Temp
Cook Time

Ingredients

Directions

Notes:

Recipe Name: _____ ☆☆☆☆☆

Nutrition Info

Serves
Prep Time
Oven Temp
Cook Time

Ingredients

Directions

Notes:

Recipe Name: _____ ☆☆☆☆☆

Nutrition Info

Ingredients

Directions

Notes:

Recipe Name: _____ ☆☆☆☆☆

Nutrition Info

Serves
Prep Time
Oven Temp
Cook Time

Ingredients

Directions

Notes:

Recipe Name: _____ ☆☆☆☆☆

Nutrition Info

Serves
Prep Time
Oven Temp
Cook Time

Ingredients

Directions

Notes:

Recipe Name: _____ ☆☆☆☆☆

Nutrition Info

Serves
Prep Time
Oven Temp
Cook Time

Ingredients

Directions

Notes:

Recipe Name: _____ ☆☆☆☆☆

Nutrition Info

Serves
Prep Time
Oven Temp
Cook Time

Ingredients

Directions

Notes:

Recipe Name: _____ ☆☆☆☆☆

Nutrition Info

Serves
Prep Time
Oven Temp
Cook Time

Ingredients

Directions

Notes:

Recipe Name: _____ ☆☆☆☆☆

Nutrition Info

Serves
Prep Time
Oven Temp
Cook Time

Ingredients

Directions

Notes:

Recipe Name: _____ ☆☆☆☆☆

Nutrition Info

Serves
Prep Time
Oven Temp
Cook Time

Ingredients

Directions

Notes:

Recipe Name: _____ ☆☆☆☆☆

Nutrition Info

Serves
Prep Time
Oven Temp
Cook Time

Ingredients

Directions

Notes:

Recipe Name: _____ ☆☆☆☆☆

Nutrition Info

Serves
Prep Time
Oven Temp
Cook Time

Ingredients

Directions

Notes:

Recipe Name: _____ ☆☆☆☆☆

Nutrition Info

Serves
Prep Time
Oven Temp
Cook Time

Ingredients

Directions

Notes:

Recipe Name: _____ ☆☆☆☆☆

Nutrition Info

Serves
Prep Time
Oven Temp
Cook Time

Ingredients

Directions

Notes:

Recipe Name: _____ ☆☆☆☆☆

Nutrition Info

Serves
Prep Time
Oven Temp
Cook Time

Ingredients

Directions

Notes:

Recipe Name: _____ ☆☆☆☆☆

Nutrition Info

Serves
Prep Time
Oven Temp
Cook Time

Ingredients

Directions

Notes:

Recipe Name: _____ ☆☆☆☆☆

Nutrition Info

Serves
Prep Time
Oven Temp
Cook Time

Ingredients

Directions

Notes:

Recipe Name: _____ ☆☆☆☆☆

Nutrition Info

Serves
Prep Time
Oven Temp
Cook Time

Ingredients

Directions

Notes:

Recipe Name: _____ ☆☆☆☆☆

Nutrition Info

Serves
Prep Time
Oven Temp
Cook Time

Ingredients

Directions

Notes:

Recipe Name: _____ ☆☆☆☆☆

Nutrition Info

Serves
Prep Time
Oven Temp
Cook Time

Ingredients

Directions

Notes:

Recipe Name: _____ ☆☆☆☆☆

Nutrition Info

Serves
Prep Time
Oven Temp
Cook Time

Ingredients

Directions

Notes:

Recipe Name: _____ ☆☆☆☆☆

Nutrition Info

Serves
Prep Time
Oven Temp
Cook Time

Ingredients

Directions

Notes:

Recipe Name: _____ ☆☆☆☆☆

Nutrition Info

Serves
Prep Time
Oven Temp
Cook Time

Ingredients

Directions

Notes:

Recipe Name: _____ ☆☆☆☆☆

Nutrition Info

Serves
Prep Time
Oven Temp
Cook Time

Ingredients

Directions

Notes:

Recipe Name: ☆☆☆☆☆

Nutrition Info

Serves
Prep Time
Oven Temp
Cook Time

Ingredients

Directions

Notes:

Recipe Name: _____ ☆☆☆☆☆

Nutrition Info

Serves

Prep Time

Oven Temp

Cook Time

Ingredients

Directions

Notes:

Recipe Name: _____ ☆☆☆☆☆

Nutrition Info

Serves
Prep Time
Oven Temp
Cook Time

Ingredients

Directions

Notes:

Recipe Name: _____ ☆☆☆☆☆

Nutrition Info

Serves
Prep Time
Oven Temp
Cook Time

Ingredients

Directions

Notes:

Recipe Name: _____ ☆☆☆☆☆

Nutrition Info

Serves
Prep Time
Oven Temp
Cook Time

Ingredients

Directions

Notes:

Recipe Name: _____ ☆☆☆☆☆

Nutrition Info

Serves
Prep Time
Oven Temp
Cook Time

Ingredients

Directions

Notes:

Recipe Name: _____ ☆☆☆☆☆

Nutrition Info

Serves
Prep Time
Oven Temp
Cook Time

Ingredients

Directions

Notes:

Recipe Name: _____ ☆☆☆☆☆

Nutrition Info

Serves
Prep Time
Oven Temp
Cook Time

Ingredients

Directions

Notes:

Recipe Name: _____ ☆☆☆☆☆

Nutrition Info

Serves
Prep Time
Oven Temp
Cook Time

Ingredients

Directions

Notes:

Recipe Name: _____ ☆☆☆☆☆

Nutrition Info

Serves
Prep Time
Oven Temp
Cook Time

Ingredients

Directions

Notes:

Recipe Name: _____ ☆☆☆☆☆

Nutrition Info

Serves
Prep Time
Oven Temp
Cook Time

Ingredients

Directions

Notes:

Recipe Name: _____ ☆☆☆☆☆

Nutrition Info

Serves
Prep Time
Oven Temp
Cook Time

Ingredients

Directions

Notes:

Recipe Name: _____ ☆☆☆☆☆

Nutrition Info

Serves
Prep Time
Oven Temp
Cook Time

Ingredients

Directions

Notes:

Recipe Name: _____ ☆☆☆☆☆

Nutrition Info

Serves
Prep Time
Oven Temp
Cook Time

Ingredients

Directions

Notes:

Recipe Name: _____ ☆☆☆☆☆

Nutrition Info

Serves
Prep Time
Oven Temp
Cook Time

Ingredients

Directions

Notes:

Recipe Name: _____ ☆☆☆☆☆

Nutrition Info

Serves
Prep Time
Oven Temp
Cook Time

Ingredients

Directions

Notes:

Recipe Name: _____

☆☆☆☆☆

Nutrition Info

Serves
Prep Time
Oven Temp
Cook Time

Ingredients

Directions

Notes:

Recipe Name: _____ ☆☆☆☆☆

Nutrition Info

Serves

Prep Time

Oven Temp

Cook Time

Ingredients

Directions

Notes:

Recipe Name: _____ ☆☆☆☆☆

Nutrition Info

Serves
Prep Time
Oven Temp
Cook Time

Ingredients

Directions

Notes:

Recipe Name: _____ ☆☆☆☆☆

Nutrition Info

Serves
Prep Time
Oven Temp
Cook Time

Ingredients

Directions

Notes:

Recipe Name: _____ ☆☆☆☆☆

Nutrition Info

Serves
Prep Time
Oven Temp
Cook Time

Ingredients

Directions

Notes:

Recipe Name: _____

☆☆☆☆☆

Nutrition Info

Serves
Prep Time
Oven Temp
Cook Time

Ingredients

Directions

Notes:

Recipe Name: _____ ☆☆☆☆☆

Nutrition Info

Serves
Prep Time
Oven Temp
Cook Time

Ingredients

Directions

Notes:

Recipe Name: _____ ☆☆☆☆☆

Nutrition Info

Serves
Prep Time
Oven Temp
Cook Time

Ingredients

Directions

Notes:

Recipe Name: ☆☆☆☆☆

Nutrition Info

Serves
Prep Time
Oven Temp
Cook Time

Ingredients

Directions

Notes:

Recipe Name: _____ ☆☆☆☆☆

Nutrition Info

Serves
Prep Time
Oven Temp
Cook Time

Ingredients

Directions

Notes:

Recipe Name: _____ ☆☆☆☆☆

Nutrition Info

Serves
Prep Time
Oven Temp
Cook Time

Ingredients

Directions

Notes:

Recipe Name: _____ ☆☆☆☆☆

Nutrition Info

Serves
Prep Time
Oven Temp
Cook Time

Ingredients

Directions

Notes:

Recipe Name: _____ ☆☆☆☆☆

Nutrition Info

Serves
Prep Time
Oven Temp
Cook Time

Ingredients

Directions

Notes:

Recipe Name: _____ ☆☆☆☆☆

Nutrition Info

Serves
Prep Time
Oven Temp
Cook Time

Ingredients

Directions

Notes:

Recipe Name: _____

☆☆☆☆☆

Nutrition Info

Serves
Prep Time
Oven Temp
Cook Time

Ingredients

Directions

Notes:

Recipe Name: _____ ☆☆☆☆☆

Nutrition Info

Serves
Prep Time
Oven Temp
Cook Time

Ingredients

Directions

Notes:

Recipe Name: _____ ☆☆☆☆☆

Nutrition Info

Serves
Prep Time
Oven Temp
Cook Time

Ingredients

Directions

Notes:

Recipe Name: _____ ☆☆☆☆☆

Nutrition Info

Serves
Prep Time
Oven Temp
Cook Time

Ingredients

Directions

Notes:

CPSIA information can be obtained
at www.ICGtesting.com
Printed in the USA
FSOW03n2134140716
22779FS